The SUMMER OLYMPICS

ON THE WORLD STAGE

FASCINATING FACTS

The SUMMER OLYMPICS

ON THE WORLD STAGE

ATHLETES TO WATCH

FASCINATING FACTS

GREATEST MOMENTS

RECORD BREAKERS

The SUMMER OLYMPICS

ON THE WORLD STAGE

FASCINATING FACTS

GREG BACH

MASON CREST

PHILADELPHIA | MIAMI

MASON CREST
450 Parkway Drive, Suite D, Broomall, Pennsylvania 19008
(866) MCP-BOOK (toll-free) • www.masoncrest.com

Printed and bound in the United States of America.

First printing

9 8 7 6 5 4 3 2 1
ISBN (hardback) 978-1-4222-4445-6
ISBN (series) 978-1-4222-4443-2
ISBN (ebook) 978-1-4222-7366-1

Library of Congress Cataloging-in-Publication Data on file at the Library of Congress.

Developed and Produced by National Highlights Inc.
Editor: Andrew Luke
Production: Crafted Content LLC

Cover images, clockwise from top left:

Olympic gold medal (Mitch Ames@Wikimedia Commons), Torch lighting during the Rio 2016 Summer Olympics (Agencia Brasil Fotografias@Wikimedia Commons), an unidentified person painting (Kutizoltan Dreamstime.com), 1980 women's field hockey team from Zimbabwe (RIA Novosti archive Vitaliy Saveliev@Wikimedia Commons)

QR CODES AND LINKS TO THIRD-PARTY CONTENT

CONTENTS

WHAT ARE THE SUMMER OLYMPICS?

The ancient Olympic Games took place in Greece every four years for nearly 12 centuries from 776 BC through 393 AD. They were part of a religious festival to honor Zeus, who was the father of Greek gods and goddesses. The event was held in Olympia, a sanctuary site named for Mount Olympus, which is the country's tallest mountain and the mythological home of the Greek gods. It is the place for which the Olympics are named.

Roughly 1,500 years after the ancient Games ended, a Frenchman named Baron Pierre de Coubertin wanted to resurrect the Olympic Games to coincide with the 1900 World Fair in Paris. The 1900 Paris Exposition was to feature the newest, modern-day, turn-of-the-century attractions like talking films, the diesel engine, escalators, magnet audio recorders, and a fairly new Eiffel Tower painted yellow.

De Coubertin wanted the best athletes in the world for the first modern Olympic Games outside of Greece, so he presented the idea in 1894. Representatives from 34 potential countries got so excited about his plan that they proposed the Games take place in 1896 instead. So, the modern Olympics, as it is now called, began where the ancient Games left off—in Athens, Greece, in 1896.

The 10-day event in April 1896 had 241 male athletes from 14 countries competing in 43 events. The events at these Athens Games were athletics (track and field), swimming, cycling, fencing, gymnastics, shooting, tennis, weightlifting, and wrestling. The ancient Games had consisted of short races, days-long boxing matches, and chariot races.

Like the ancient Games, organizers held the event every four years, with Paris hosting in 1900, when women made their first appearance. The Paris Games had many more competitors, as 997 athletes represented 24 countries in 95 total events. These Games were spread out from May through October to coincide with the Paris Exposition.

The Summer Olympics have now spanned into the 21st century and have become the ultimate crowning achievement for athletes worldwide. The Games have evolved with the addition and removal of events, the scope of media coverage, the addition of a separate Winter Olympics, and the emergence of both the Special Olympics and Paralympic Games.

The Olympics have been the site of great athletic feats and sportsmanship. They have presented tragedy, triumph, controversy, and political grandstanding. There have been legendary athletes, remarkable human-interest stories, doping allegations, boycotts, terrorist attacks, and three cancellations because of worldwide war.

Yet the Olympics, with its five interlocking rings and eternal flame, remain a symbol of unity and hope.

The United States hosted its first Games in 1904 in St. Louis, Missouri, which, like Paris, spread the Games over several months in conjunction with the World Fair. The presentation of gold, silver, and bronze medals for finishing first, second, and third in each event began at this Olympics.

More than 2,000 athletes competed in England at the 1908 London Games, which were originally scheduled for Rome but reassigned once organizers discovered the Italian capital would not be ready in time. In London, the marathon race was extended by 195 meters so the finish line would be just below the royal box in the stadium and thus the 26.2 miles from the 1908 edition went on to become the official marathon distance beginning with the 1924 Paris Games.

Stockholm, Sweden, hosted the 1912 Games, and the Olympics were cancelled in 1916 because of World War I (WWI). Other years in which the Olympic Games were not held include 1940 and 1944 because of World War II.

Berlin, Germany, had been awarded the 1916 Olympics that were cancelled, but rather than reward the Germans following WWI by giving them the 1920 Games, they were instead awarded to Antwerp, Belgium, to honor the Belgians who suffered so many hardships during the war. The Olympic flag, which shows five interlocked rings to signify the universality of the Games, was first hoisted during the 1920 opening ceremonies in Antwerp. The Olympic rings have become a well-known symbol of sportsmanship and unity worldwide.

The 1924 Games were back in Paris, and the Olympics became a recognized, bona fide worldwide event. The number of participating countries went from 29 to 44. There were more than 3,000 athletes competing and more than 1,000 journalists covering the competition.

Also, in 1924, the annual event became known as the Summer Olympics, or Summer Games, as the Winter Olympics debuted in Chamonix, France. The Winter Games were held every four years through 1992. The Winter Olympics were then held again in 1994 and every four years since then.

Two more long-standing traditions began at the 1928 Summer Games in Amsterdam, Netherlands. The Olympic flame was lit for the first time in a cauldron at the top of the Olympic stadium. Also, during the opening ceremony, the national team of Greece entered the stadium first and the Dutch entered last, signifying the first team to host the modern Olympics and the current host. This tradition still stands today.

The United States got its second Summer Olympics in 1932, when Los Angeles, California, hosted. The city built a lavish coliseum for the Games, and it was the last time the USA would host the Summer Olympics for 52 years, when they were once again held in Los Angeles in 1984, at the same stadium.

The 1936 Summer Olympics in Berlin also produced some long-lasting, first-time traditions. These Games were the first to have a torch relay bringing the Olympic flame to the stadium, and they were also the first to be televised.

The Summer Olympics took a 12-year hiatus because of World War II, and London was once again called upon to host the Games with short notice in 1948.

The Summer Games have been held every four years since 1948. In 2016, Rio de Janeiro, Brazil, hosted the Summer Games, and that meant the Olympics had now been held on five continents. Australia has hosted the Summer Olympics twice (Melbourne in 1956 and Sydney in 2000). Asia has hosted four times (Tokyo, Japan in 1964 and 2020; Seoul, Korea, in 1988; and Beijing, China, in 2008).

Other North American cities to host the Summer Olympics have been Mexico City, Mexico, in 1968; Montreal, Canada, in 1976; and Atlanta, Georgia, in 1996 for the centennial anniversary of the modern Olympics. Los Angeles will host the Games for a third time in 2028.

Although athletes typically garner headlines for most Olympic coverage, sometimes events outside of the playing field force the world to take notice.

Eight Palestinian terrorists shot two Israeli athletes dead and held nine more as hostages during the 1972 Munich Games in Germany. Those nine were also murdered during a botched rescue attempt.

The 1980 Moscow Games in Russia saw the fewest number of athletes in a Summer Olympics since 1956, when the USA led a boycott of Moscow after the Soviet Union invaded Afghanistan in December of 1979.

The Soviet Union then led a contingency of Eastern European nations that boycotted the 1984 Los Angeles Games during the Cold War, mainly as payback for the U.S. boycott.

The first Summer Olympics that were boycott-free since 1972 were the 1992 Games in Barcelona, Spain, which was also the first time professional basketball players competed, opening the door for professionals in all Olympic sports except wrestling and boxing. Before the International Olympic Committee (IOC) approved professional athletes to participate in the late 1980s, the Olympics were primarily for the world's best amateur athletes.

Many have lamented the demise of amateurism at the Olympic Games, but by far the most contentious issue the IOC has dealt with in recent years is the scourge of steroids and other prohibited performance-enhancing drugs.

The world's greatest celebration of sport has had a checkered and colorful past, from politics and doping to sheer athleticism and the triumph of the human spirit. This century has seen the Summer Games return to familiar places (Athens 2004, London 2012) and expand to new ones (Sydney 2000, Rio de Janeiro 2016). Tokyo awaits the world in 2020, when the newest great Olympic stories will be told.

– Scott McDonald, Olympic and Paralympic Journalist

FASCINATING FACTS

Throughout the rich and glorious history of the Summer Olympics, there have been many fascinating, unusual, and downright quirky moments that have taken place before, during, and after events. In *Fascinating Facts*, part of the four-title *The Summer Olympics: On the World Stage* series, we dive into the heroic and horrific, as well as the outrageous and obscure, providing eye-opening accounts of some of the both amazing and incredibly wacky moments that have made the Games a global showcase.

There's Bill Hoyt, an American college student who had to fake an illness to compete at the first modern Olympic Games—the 1896 Summer Games in Athens; Robert LeGendre, who set a world record in the long jump at the 1924 Games, but didn't take home a gold medal; the eight badminton players who were kicked out of the 2012 Games in London for intentionally losing matches; gymnast George Eyser, who won six medals while competing with a wooden leg; and marathon runner Fred Lorz, who hitched a ride in a car during the race and hopped out to run the final couple of miles to cross the finish line first. All these stories—plus a 10-year-old boy who competed at the 1896 Summer Games, a 72-year-old Swede who won a medal at the 1920 Antwerp Games, the boxing official who was attacked in the ring, the debut of Waldi (the first official mascot of an Olympic Games), and much more—are here.

Fascinating Facts takes you on a journey through Olympic history that will shock, entertain, and enlighten along the way.

ADOLESCENT ACROBAT FACT #1

10-Year-Old Competed in 1896 Summer Games

Throughout the glorious history of the Olympic Games, legions of adolescent athletes have amazed and thrilled with performances that are often hard to fathom coming from such young people and small bodies. At the inaugural modern Olympic Games—hosted in Athens, Greece, in 1896—a 10-year-old Greek boy named Dimitrios Loundras competed in gymnastics in the team parallel bars event. He was the youngest to participate in Athens, and more than a century later he still owns the distinction of being the Olympic Games' youngest competitor ever.

Three teams (two from Greece and one from Germany) comprised of four gymnasts each took part in the team parallel bars event. Loundras competed as part of the Ethnikos Gymnastikos Syllogos team that placed third, while Germany won the event.

Ever since Loundras' appearance, many athletes not much older than him have savored Olympic glory. Eleven-year-old Luigina Giavotti was the youngest medalist at

LOUNDRAS' LABOR OF LOVE

Later in life, Loundras was a member of the Hellenic Olympic Committee, which worked with other sport federations to spread the Olympic spirit. He also played a prominent role in forming the Hellenic Shooting Federation, an umbrella organization for sport shooting in Greece, and served as its first president.

the 1928 Summer Olympics in Amsterdam, as she was part of the Italian team that won a silver medal in the gymnastics team competition. In diving, American Marjorie Gestring won a gold medal at the 1936 Games as a 13-year-old in the springboard event in Berlin, and at the 1992 Barcelona Games, Chinese diving sensation Fu Mingxia won a gold medal at the age of 13 in the 10-meter platform event. And who can ever forget 14-year-old Nadia Comăneci earning the first perfect 10 in gymnastics at the 1976 Games in Montreal.

YOUNGEST TO OLDEST

Prior to his death in 1970, Loundras was the last surviving participant from the 1896 Summer Olympics in Athens. This was no mean feat, as he spent much of his life in the Royal Hellenic Navy, reaching the rank of rear admiral. Loundras fought in World War I against the Germans and against the Italians in World War II.

SUPER SENIOR FACT #2

72-Year-Old Wins Olympic Medal

When it comes to the Olympic Games, it is certainly no secret that 20- and 30-somethings in the prime of their athletic lives corral the bulk of the medals. And that makes what Sweden's Oscar Swahn pulled off during a 12-year-stretch—deep into his life—all the more remarkable.

Swahn made his Olympic debut in shooting at the age of 60 at the 1908 Games in London and took advantage of his keen eyesight and quick reflexes to win three medals, two of them gold. He won the running deer single-shot event and the next day helped Sweden win the single-shot team event. Swahn also won bronze in the double-shot event. Shooters stood 110 yards (100.58 meters) away from a deer-shaped target that moved across a 75-foot run in the span of about 4 seconds.

Swahn returned to the Olympics in 1912 at the Stockholm Games, where he won a bronze in the double-shot and a gold medal in the team single-shot competition, becoming the oldest gold medalist of all time at the age of 64. But it turned out that he wasn't done setting age records, or winning medals, just yet.

SHOT SELECTION

The targets used during the running deer events featured three circles that competitors aimed at. The smallest of the circles was worth four points, the middle was worth three points, and the outermost circle earned two points. If a shooter hit the target but not a circle, they were awarded a point, except if they hit haunch (butt and thigh), which received no points.

In 1920, at the age of 72, Swahn competed in his third Olympic Games in Antwerp, earning him the distinction of being the oldest-ever competing Olympian, as well as the oldest to claim an Olympic medal. He competed in three events, winning a silver medal in the running deer double-shot team event.

Swahn qualified for the 1924 Olympics as well, but did not participate due to illness.

FATHER AND SON

Oscar competed alongside his son Alfred during the Olympics. Alfred was a great shooter just like his dad. Alfred competed in four Olympics (three with his dad) and won nine medals, three of them gold. The Swahns shared the team gold medal in single-shot running deer in both 1908 and 1912.

THAT SINKING FEELING
FACT #3

Ali's 1960 Gold Medal Mysteriously "Disappeared"

In 1960, Cassius Clay (who would later be called Muhammad Ali, the great showman and champion), was a supremely talented amateur boxer from Louisville, Kentucky. A six-time Golden Gloves winner in his home state, Clay made the Olympic team for his country and was the clear favorite to win the gold medal in the light heavyweight division.

The 18-year-old Clay did not disappoint, winning gold with three unanimous decisions and a TKO (technical knockout). Clay was so proud of his win that he wore the medal around his neck for days after arriving back home in Louisville. On one of those days, he and a friend tried to get service at a local restaurant, but back then, in a racially segregated Louisville, they were refused any service. This part of the story is not in dispute.

Where the story takes on the mantle of urban legend is that after leaving the restaurant, Clay was supposedly so angry and frustrated that he threw his medal off the Second Street Bridge in protest and it sank to the bottom of the Ohio River.

This account first appeared in Ali's 1975 autobiography, but when Ali was asked about it later, he refused—and continued refusing up until his death in 2016—to confirm that this actually happened. Close friends of his have insisted the medal meant too much to Ali for him to throw it away. It has also been speculated that the medal was lost when he was moving.

Whatever the case may be, the medal was lost, and the International Olympic Committee (IOC) honored Ali at the 1996 Atlanta Games by presenting him with a replacement.

FLIGHT OR FIGHT

Clay almost skipped the Olympics in 1960 because he was so afraid of flying. He asked if he could go by sea, but there was no time for that. It took a long, face-to-face talk with Joe Martin to convince Clay to go. Martin was Clay's first trainer; the man who taught him to fight when Clay was 12 years old so that he could stand up to the boy who stole his bicycle.

"Champions aren't made in the gyms. Champions are made from something they have deep inside them – a desire, a dream, a vision."

— Cassius Clay

MARATHON MAYHEM FACT #4

American Wins Marathon Running Just 14 Miles

The 1904 Olympic marathon had more bizarre twists and scary moments than a Stephen King novel. The shenanigans around the race included blatant cheating, drugs, wild animals, and the most unusual cast of runners to ever participate in the grueling event. Among the field of 32 runners in St. Louis were 10 Greeks running their first marathon, two shoeless South Africans, a Cuban wearing a long sleeve shirt and long pants in the sweltering heat, and a group of five strong American distance runners.

The dusty, hilly course forced runners to navigate everything from delivery wagons to railroad trains, and at one point a runner was chased off course by a pack of not-so-friendly dogs. The punishing heat struck hard, forcing several runners to drop out, including American William Garcia, who nearly died due to a stomach hemorrhage. When cramps hit Fred Lorz at the 9-mile mark he hitched a ride in a car—and was even seen waving at runners and spectators as he rode past them. American Thomas Hicks, one of the pre-race favorites, began struggling 7 miles from the finish and was given the drug strychnine, which was used in small doses as a stimulant in those days.

Lorz hopped out of the car 5 miles from the finish line and resumed running, crossing the finish line first to a cheering crowd. That applause turned to boos when it was learned he had cheated. He admitted it, saying he was only joking. Hicks won the gold medal as only 14 runners completed the race.

> **"Never in my life have I run such a tough course. The terrific hills simply tear a man to pieces."**
> **— Thomas Hicks**

The 1904 Olympic marathon in St. Louis was one of the strangest races ever, which included one runner hitching a ride in an automobile and another consuming strychnine.

STROLLING FOR GLORY
FACT #5

Athletes Can Win Olympic Medals by Walking

There are lots of paths to the Olympic medal podium: athletes can wind up there by excelling at running, jumping, swimming, diving, tumbling, cycling, and hurdling, to name a few. As it turns out, one can get there by walking too. That's right, racewalking is an Olympic sport that has been around since the early 1900s for men in various forms. These days, men compete in 20-kilometer (12.4 miles) and 50-kilometer (31 miles) races, while women compete in a 20-kilometer race, which was added to the Olympic lineup for the first time at the 1992 Summer Games in Barcelona.

By keeping their arms tight to their bodies and constantly pumping, blended with short and quick strides, athletes generate both power and speed in this sport. This results in an odd-looking wiggling stride. Two key rules: the leading leg must be straight when it contacts the ground and remain that way until it's lifted again and competitors must have at least one foot touching the ground at all times. Race judges watch for rules infractions and issue red cards as warnings for violations. Competitors who receive three red cards are disqualified.

At the 2016 Games in Rio, the most thrilling race was the women's 20 kilometers, where China's Hong Liu held off Mexico's Maria Guadalupe Gonzalez by 2 seconds to win gold with a time of 1:28:35. China's Zhen Wang won gold in the men's 20 kilometers with a time of 1:19:14 and Slovakia's Matej Toth was the first to cross the finish line in the 50 kilometers in 3:40:58.

AMERICA'S RACEWALKING GREAT

Larry Young was the last American to win an Olympic medal in racewalking, taking third in the 50-kilometer races at the 1968 Games in Mexico City and the 1972 Games in Munich. He won 30 national titles during his illustrious career and was inducted into the USA Track and Field Hall of Fame in 2002.

Russia's Elena Lashmanova won the women's 20-kilometer racewalking at the 2012 Olympics in London.

FROM OFFICE TO PODIUM
FACT #6

Bookkeeper Turns Gold Medalist in 47 Days

The U.S.-led boycott of the 1980 Summer Games in Moscow smothered the lifelong dreams of many athletes who were denied the opportunity to compete. About 7,000 miles away in Zimbabwe, though, it nudged open the door for an unlikely group of women to rock the Olympic landscape.

The boycott depleted many events, including women's field hockey where the Soviet team was the only one remaining. Olympic authorities resorted to filling the open spots by inviting teams from countries that had not qualified earlier. Zimbabwe received its invite 35 days before the opening ceremonies and quickly patched together a team that would compete overseas for the first time ever.

Ann Grant, a 25-year-old bookkeeper and an experienced field hockey player, was tabbed as the team captain for Zimbabwe. She led the group, which featured women who had been busy with occupations such as secretaries, clerks, and homemakers, into Moscow and onto an artificial turf surface that they had never played on before. The strange surface and lack of practice time didn't affect their play as this makeshift team

POWER PLAY

U.S. President Jimmy Carter boycotted the Moscow Games in response to the Soviet invasion of Afghanistan in 1979. Canada, West Germany, and Japan were among 65 nations who did not compete. The presidential announcement came after the Soviet Union failed to comply with Carter's deadline of February 20, 1980, to withdraw its troops from Afghanistan.

opened with a 4—0 win over Poland. They also shut out the Soviet team 2—0 and played India and Czechoslovakia to ties, setting up a gold medal showdown with Austria.

The Zimbabweans and the Austrians were even at 1—1 following the first half. The second half proved to be a showcase of great play from Zimbabwe, which scored three times and won 4—1 to claim gold. Grant's teammates carried her off the field on their shoulders.

LONE GOLD

The only medal Zimbabwe won at the 1980 Summer Games was its gold in women's field hockey. This is despite the fact that the Zimbabwean team in 1980 is the biggest team the country has ever sent to any Olympic games. Zimbabwe has three total gold medals in its Olympic history, also winning one gold in each of 2004 and 2008. Swimmer Kirsty Coventry won both, part of her total of seven Olympic medals.

POST-FIGHT FURY
FACT #7

Boxing Referee Assaulted at Seoul Games

Some of the most vicious punches landed during the boxing competition at the 1988 Summer Games in Seoul came from the hands of an angry mob—coaches, officials, and fans—that put a referee's safety in jeopardy and stands as one of the ugliest moments in Olympic history. A bantamweight fight between Bulgaria's Alexander Khristov and South Korea's Byun Jong-il dissolved into a shoving and grabbing match in which referee Keith Walker deducted a point from the host country's Byun in both the first and second rounds for leading with his head in a fight he would lose 4—1.

When the decision was announced, angry Korean coaches began assaulting Walker in the ring while several outraged fans also climbed over the ropes to get at him. He suffered punches to his chest and gut as he was knocked around the ring before other officials stepped in to help protect him from the swarm of violence. They helped escort him out of the arena while trying to dodge punches, jabs, and kicks from angry onlookers. By the time he got to his hotel so that he could book the first flight possible out of the country, death threats were already being made against his life.

The 19-year-old Byun, who was expected to contend for a gold medal, sat in the ring in protest for more than an hour, refusing to leave. No one removed Byun, so no other bouts could be staged. Officials postponed the remaining fights that day and turned the lights off in the arena with Byun still in the ring.

"It was absolutely diabolical. To say I feared for my life, well, I don't think I did – but I was quite terrified about who was going to clobber me next and how I was going to get clobbered."
— Keith Walker

Korean officials and fans, upset with a decision in a bantamweight fight at the 1988 Seoul Olympics, attacked boxing referee Keith Walker in one of the ugliest moments in the history of the Summer Games.

ROYAL REQUEST
FACT #8

British Monarchy Made the Marathon Longer

Competitors in the marathon at the 1908 London Olympics received an unwanted surprise, courtesy of the British monarchy: more yards to run on an already punishing journey. In the three previous Olympic marathons, runners covered between 24 and 26 miles (38.6 and 41.8 kilometers). However, the extra distance for this race was tacked on due to Queen Alexandria's excitement for the event.

The marathon was originally set to start on a street outside Windsor Castle, but the queen wanted her children to see the spectacle, so the start was shifted inside the grounds of the castle and just outside the nursery. That change, coupled with a modification at the end of the race to move the finish line in front of the queen's seats in the stadium, extended the marathon to its longest distance ever, and became the standard for the current distance used today (26.22 miles or 42.2 kilometers).

It turned out to be a memorable race. Italy's Dorando Pietri assumed the lead of the race with 2 miles (3.22 kilometers) to go, and as he entered the stadium for the final lap, his world faded

MANY MILES INSIDE MADISON SQUARE GARDEN

Two months after the Olympic marathon, Pietri and Hayes competed against each other in an indoor marathon at Madison Square Garden, where a packed arena watched them run 262 laps around an indoor track. Pietri won the race by about half a lap and beat Hayes' Olympic gold medal-winning time by almost 11 minutes.

into haziness. Overwhelmed by pain and unable to summon the strength needed to reach the finish line, he collapsed. The course clerk and chief medical officer rushed to his aid, and they and others assisted him to the finish line. When American Johnny Hayes finished the race in second, he lodged an appeal and Pietri was disqualified for being assisted around the track, giving Hayes the gold.

WHAT'S IN A NAME?

The marathon gets its name from the story of Greek messenger Pheidippides, who ran that distance from Marathon to Athens to announce a Greek victory over the Persians at the Battle of Marathon in 490 BC. Upon delivering the news, he is said to have collapsed and died.

CENTENARIAN CONFESSION FACT #9

Diver Hid Stolen Flag for 77 years

The whereabouts of the official Olympic flag of the 1920 Games in Antwerp, Belgium, was a mystery for 77 years to all but one man. USA Olympic diver Harry Prieste had not given the flag much thought over three quarters of a century, but it was he, on a dare from teammate and Olympic champion swimmer Duke Kahanamoku, who scaled the flagpole and swiped the banner as the Games ended.

What Prieste did not realize all those years is that this flag was the first to depict the now iconic symbol of the Games, the Olympic rings. The only reason the world learned he had the flag is because the subject of its disappearance happened to come up during an interview he was giving in 1997 at a United States Olympic Committee dinner. The 101-year-old Prieste stopped the reporter and said, "I can help you with that. It's in my suitcase."

Prieste, who won a bronze medal in Antwerp on the 10-meter platform, agreed to return the flag, and three years later he was honored at a dinner before the 2000 Sydney Games for giving it back, his prank forgiven. Prieste, who was a vaudeville performer and silent movie stuntman after his diving career, gave the flag to IOC president Juan Antonio Samaranch, who put it on display in the Olympic museum in Switzerland.

The flag is somewhat faded and frayed after having been inside Prieste's suitcase for 77 years. He was the oldest living American Olympian at the time he returned the flag. Prieste died in 2001 at age 104.

CALL ME HAL

Harry Prieste was not his real name, although that is the name under which he competed at the Olympics. His real first name was Haig, but he went by Harry, and then later switched to Hal. The plaque beside the flag in the Swiss museum has his stage name—Hal Haig Prieste.

"I ain't going to be around long. I had it a long time. A lot of my friends have seen it. You can't be selfish about these things. It's no good to me. I can't hang it in my room. People will think more of me by giving it away than by keeping It."

— **Hal Haig Prieste**

DOUBLE DOSE
FACT #10

Eagan Won Gold in Both Olympic Seasons

Eddie Eagan, one of the greatest amateur boxers of his era, deployed savage hands and bone-jarring power to win Olympic gold in 1920. Coupled with what he did on a patch of ice and snow years later during a New York winter, he secured the rarest Olympic achievement, one that has never been matched.

Eagan plowed through the light heavyweight division at the 1920 Amsterdam Games, handily winning all three of his fights. He dispatched Norway's three-time Olympian and two-time medalist Sverre Sørsdal in the gold medal bout. The Olympic champ returned to school at Yale University, graduating the following year, and headed to law school at Harvard University. Although he continued to fight on occasion as an amateur, when the Paris Games arrived in 1924, Eagan's ring dominance had vanished and he was beaten in his first fight.

Finished with boxing, Eagan settled into the life of an attorney until receiving a phone call that would turn

CHASING EDDIE'S EXCELLENCE

American Lauryn Williams has come the closest to joining Eagan. She won a gold medal at the 2012 Summer Games in London as part of the victorious 4x100-meter women's relay team and two years later in Sochi, Russia, at the 2014 Winter Olympics she won a silver medal in the two-woman bobsled—missing out on a gold medal by just 0.10 second.

out to be a prelude to history. He was invited to compete on a U.S. four-man bobsled team at the 1932 Winter Olympics in Lake Placid, New York. The team needed a strong body to help with the critical push off at the start of races. Having never been in a bobsled before, he quickly adapted and his team posted the fastest times in the field in three of the four runs to win the gold medal and earn Eagan the honor of being the only athlete to win a gold medal in both the Summer and Winter Games.

HALL WORTHY

Eagan was a member of the first class of athletes to be inducted into the U.S. Olympic and Paralympic Hall of Fame in 1983 along with Muhammad Ali, Jesse Owens, Bob Beamon, Peggy Fleming, Mark Spitz, and other greats. By 2019, the hall had 109 individual member athletes.

TWO CONTINENTS, ONE OLYMPICS FACT #11

Equestrian Events Held 9,704 Miles Away

The opening event of the 1956 Summer Olympics—hosted for the first time in the Southern Hemisphere in Melbourne, Australia— actually got under way eight time zones and 9,704 miles away in Stockholm, Sweden. That's where the equestrian events of dressage, show jumping, and eventing were held for more than 150 days before the world gathered in Australia to vie for gold medals in dozens of other sports.

This massive scheduling quirk marks the only time in Olympic history that events for a single Summer Games have been held on different continents.

When the IOC awarded the Games to Melbourne, one crucially important law had been overlooked in the process: they weren't aware that Australia had a strict six-month quarantine period for horses entering the country. That piece of legislation was impractical for equestrian competitors worldwide, and when Australian authorities wouldn't budge on

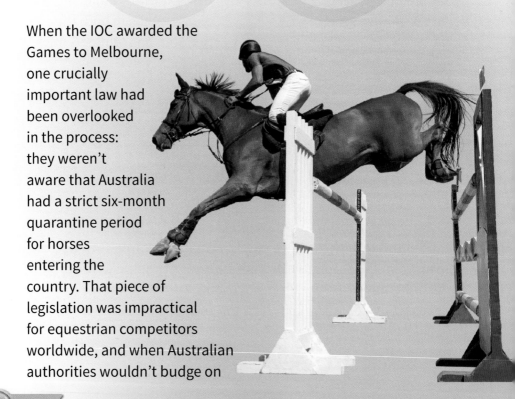

ELECTION FOR EQUESTRIAN

When Australian authorities refused to relax the quarantine laws on horses entering the country, officials from five cities volunteered to host the equestrian events: Stockholm, Los Angeles, Paris, Berlin, and Rio de Janeiro. Stockholm was the runaway winner in voting done by IOC members, while Paris was second.

adjusting it, the IOC was forced to find another location. So more than 150 competitors from more than two dozen countries headed to the Northern Hemisphere in mid-June for what many referred to as the Stockholm Equestrian Olympic Games. Swedish equestrian Hans Wikne lit the cauldron for the opening ceremonies while on horseback, the first time that had ever been done.

When the remainder of the events were held months later in Melbourne, spectators were treated to wonderful performances in many events—just not equestrian.

FAR FROM HOME

Australia, the host country for the 1956 Summer Olympics, sent four riders to compete in the equestrian events in Stockholm, Sweden. None of them won a medal. In front of their home fans, Swedish riders won three of the six equestrian events: individual and team dressage and individual eventing.

RUNNING BAREFOOT
FACT #12

Ethiopian Wins 1960 Marathon Running without Shoes

Abebe Bikila almost did not go to Rome for the 1960 Olympics. The 28-year-old long distance runner did not initially make Ethiopia's Olympic team. His teammate Wami Biratu, however, broke his ankle playing soccer and Abebe got the call that he was going to Rome with barely enough time to catch the flight.

One of the first things Abebe did when he go to Rome was to buy himself a new pair of running shoes. When race day rolled around on September 10th, however, the shoes were still giving him blisters, so he made the decision to simply run without them. When the barefooted Abebe lined up for the late afternoon start at the Piazza di Campidoglio, he was conspicuous due to being shoeless.

Abebe quickly proved that his lack of footwear was not an issue, racing from the front, and then eventually breaking away from the lead pack with Morocco's Rhadi Ben Abdessalam at about the 16-mile (26 kilometers) mark. The two men ran the next 10 miles (16 kilometers) together, until Abebe pulled away in the final 1,000 meters (0.6 miles), winning the gold medal by a comfortable 200-meter margin, blister-free bare feet and all.

The Summer Olympics: Fascinating Facts

It is often noted that Abebe made his move against the Moroccan as the runners passed the Obelisk of Axum, a monument that Italian soldiers stole from Ethiopia during the occupation of that country in World War II. His coach, Onni Niskanen, noted the landmark as the spot Abebe should sprint for the finish. He broke the world record in the victory.

EVEN BETTER WITH SHOES

Abebe returned to the Olympic games to defend his marathon gold medal at Tokyo in 1964. For an Ethiopian national hero, it was easy to get a pair of good-fitting running shoes. Abebe's choice of shoes turned out to be perfect, as he won the gold medal with a new world record time of 2:12:11.2. He was the first man to win consecutive Olympic marathons.

Watch as Abebe becomes the first East African athlete to win an Olympic medal, and the first multiple marathon winner.

MASCOT DEBUT
FACT #13

First Official Olympic Mascot a Dachshund

The Games of the XX Olympiad in Munich, Germany, in 1972, featured lots of firsts: Saudi Arabia and North Korea were among the 11 nations making their Olympic debuts; slalom canoeing was contested for the first time; and Waldi debuted as the first official Olympic mascot.

This colorful dachshund (which is a beloved animal in Germany) was chosen because that breed possesses qualities like tenacity and agility that athletes need to compete. Waldi was modeled after a real long-haired dachshund that Willi Daume, the Munich Games Organizing Committee President, had given to the International Sports Press Association President in 1970.

Waldi appeared on everything from buttons and posters to stickers and pins. The route for the marathon also resembled Waldi's shape.

Waldi's presence set in motion one of the many challenging and fun decisions that host nations are now presented with in the lead-up to the Games: deciding on a mascot. Through the years there have been many interesting characters that have pranced in front of television cameras at the opening and closing ceremonies, as well as entertained

DACHSHUND DESIGNER

The lead designer of Waldi was Otl Aicher, whose fingerprints can be found on many interesting projects: he created the logo for Lufthansa, the largest airline in Germany; he designed the Rotis typeface; and he co-founded the Ulm School of Design for college students interested in pursuing design work.

children outside venues throughout the Games. For instance, at the 2016 Rio Games there was Vinicius, a colorful mix of six different Brazilian animals; at the 1992 Barcelona Games, it was a Pyrenean mountain dog named Cobi; at the 1980 Moscow Games, it was a bear named Misha; and at the 1984 Games in Los Angeles, the official mascot was an eagle named Sam.

ETERNAL FUTURE

When the world gathers for the 2020 Games in Tokyo, they will be greeted by a mascot named Miraitowa, a name obtained from the Japanese words *mirai* (future) and *towa* (eternity), picked to promote eternal hope worldwide. The character was created by Japanese artist Ryo Taniguchi.

TAKING THE PLUNGE
FACT #14

Floating Face Down was an Olympic Sport

One of the slowest moving sports of all time made one of the fastest exits from the Summer Games' lineup. The sport of plunging debuted at the 1904 Summer Olympics in St. Louis—only five Americans competed in the event—and it was never held at another Olympiad again. The peculiar sport involved competitors standing at the edge of a pool, diving in, and remaining face down and still in the water for one minute. Whoever floated the furthest was declared the winner.

William Dickey gained the distinction of winning the only Olympic gold medal ever handed out in the sport, as his winning plunge was 62 feet 6 inches (19.05 meters). Dickey's teammates Edgar Adams (17.52 meters or 57.5 feet) and Leo Goodwin (17.37 meters or 57 feet) claimed the silver and bronze medals, respectively. Goodwin also won a gold medal for water polo in St. Louis. Newman Samuels was fourth in the plunging event (16.76 meters or 55 feet) and Charles Pyrah, the American record holder at the time, finished last in the field with a plunge of 13.97 meters (45.8 feet). All three medalists competed on the New York Athletic Club swimming team.

Dickey's golden Olympic plunge didn't come close to threatening the world record for a 60-second limit

SPARTAN PLUNGING

Plunging is not extinct, as it still takes place around the globe and in the United States. The Michigan State University men's and women's swimming teams conduct the event as one of many fun activities that are a part of their annual alumni swim meet on campus where current and former Spartans give it a try.

competition of 79 feet 3 inches (24.15 meters).

With modest athletic ability required to compete, and little spectator interest in watching competitors float while remaining motionless, the sport was sunk. It never gained traction, especially among elite swimmers or divers, and by the 1920s it had been erased from most U.S. swimming competitions.

19TH CENTURY FUN

While plunging's origins are murky, the Swimming Association of Great Britain was conducting plunging championships in the early 1880s. At its one and only Olympic appearance at the 1904 Olympics in St. Louis, plunging was categorized as a diving event.

Floating Face Down was an Olympic Sport

COURAGEOUS DISMOUNT FACT #15

Fujimoto Wins Gold Medal with Broken Knee

In one of the greatest displays of courage and grit to ever grace the Olympic Games, Japan's Shun Fujimoto performed a twisting double somersault dismount from the rings apparatus and stuck the landing—and he did so with a broken kneecap. That routine, which also tore ligaments in his leg when he landed and knocked him out of the competition, inspired his teammates to go on and win Japan's fifth straight gold medal in the team event in men's gymnastics at the 1976 Summer Games in Montreal.

Earlier in the competition Fujimoto had broken his kneecap while tumbling during his floor exercise routine, but he somehow managed to hide his agony and remarkably continued competing. Japan had entered as the favorites in the team competition and Fujimoto didn't want to let his teammates down. Plus, with their rival the Soviet Union looking to end its streak of four straight Olympics finishing with silver medals around their necks, he knew how crucial it was for him to deliver big point-producing routines.

Following the floor exercise, Fujimoto tallied a 9.5 on the pommel horse and then moved onto the diabolical rings, where he knew a pain-filled landing awaited. His dismount to cap off a terrific routine was accompanied by a grimace, a slight knee buckle, a 9.7 score, and a spot in Olympic history as one of the bravest performances ever seen. Of course, Fujimoto managed to walk himself to the podium to receive his team gold medal.

"Although I was injured, I had to do it anyway – for me, for the team. I didn't want to say anything to my team about my leg. I didn't want to upset them."
— Shun Fujimoto

Shun Fujimoto helped Japan win a gold medal in men's gymnastics at the 1976 Summer Games in Montreal while competing with a broken knee.

ONE-LEGGED LEGEND
FACT #16

Gymnast Wins Six Medals with Wooden Leg

George Eyser suffered unimaginable tragedy in his youth, but somehow flipped the script on a life destined for struggle and anonymity by later triumphing at the Olympic Games with performances bordering on unbelievable. At the age of 14, after moving with his family from Germany to the United States, he was involved in an accident in which a train hit him, resulting in his left leg being amputated above the knee.

Equipped with a prosthetic built out of wood and leather, Eyser began showing up at a local gymnastics club near his home, where he fell in love with the sport. When the Summer Games arrived in St. Louis in 1904, he was an eager participant. These Games were conducted alongside the World's Fair, so the events were oddly scattered throughout the year. In July, some gymnastics events were held, where Eyser understandably struggled. In the all-around competition, which back then included the 100-yard dash and long jump among several events, Eyser finished in 71st place.

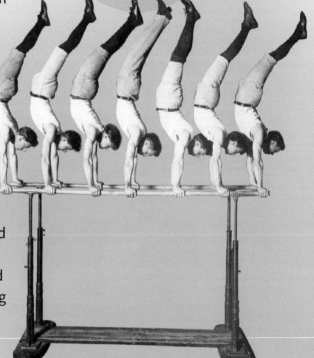

PRECEDENT-SETTING PERFORMANCE

South African swimmer Natalie du Toit was hit by a car at age 17 and had her left leg amputated at the knee. Like Eyser, her accident didn't ruin her dreams. She was the first female amputee to qualify for the Olympics and she finished in 16th place in the women's 10-kilometer open water race at the 2008 Games, competing with no prosthetic assistance.

Three months later, when the more traditional events of gymnastics were contested, Eyser turned in a stunning display. He won three gold medals, winning the parallel bars, rope climbing, and tying with Anton Heida for first in the men's vault. He also won silver medals in the pommel horse and in the men's combined and a bronze on the horizontal bar. Going against able-bodied competitors, Eyser's effort embodied what the Olympic spirit is all about.

FOREIGN BORN

Eyser competed for the United States, but he was actually born in Germany. He became a U.S. citizen in 1894 at age 24. Intent on competing in the Olympics, he moved to St. Louis from Denver, Colorado, not long before the 1904 Games. Eyser did not compete at the 1908 Games in London.

"SICK" LEAVE
FACT #17

Harvard Student Fakes Illness to Win Olympic Event

While Harvard sophomore Bill Hoyt was launching himself into the air during the pole vault competition at the 1896 Summer Olympics in Greece, school officials assumed he was bedridden at his home in Massachusetts recovering from a nasty illness. Charles William Elliott, the president of Harvard University, wasn't a big fan of athletic competition. In the months leading up to the Games in Greece he granted one student a leave of absence to participate—and it wasn't Hoyt. So Hoyt faked an illness, withdrew from school, and joined the contingent of American athletes that set sail from New Jersey.

Hoyt certainly made the most of his fake illness by winning the pole vault, outperforming American Albert Tyler, a member of the Princeton football team. The field of five competitors included three Greeks, who all failed to clear 7 feet 7 inches (2.31 meters) and were quickly eliminated. When the bar reached 10 feet (3.05 meters), Hoyt missed on his first two attempts while Tyler cleared it with

FOUNDING FATHERS

Hoyt was one of 14 men who spent 17 days at sea and on trains to reach Greece for the Olympic Games. He, along with most of the others, either represented the Boston Athletic Association track team or were students from Princeton University. This group is often referred to as the "Founding Fathers of Team USA." Together they won a total of 11 events.

ease. Hoyt's final attempt was a success, keeping him in the competition. He went on to clear 10 feet 9¾ inches (3.3 meters), which earned him first place.

Hoyt returned to Harvard, where he had "recovered" from his lengthy illness and graduated in 1897. Four years later he earned a degree from Harvard's medical school and served as a surgeon on the Western Front in France during World War I. He later worked as a surgeon for the U.S. Public Health Service.

ROUGH LANDING

Pole vaulting was a rough and tumble sport at the 1896 Games as there wasn't a cushy pit to fall into on the landing—only the hard ground. Today large foam mats 1 to 1.5 meters (3 feet to 4 feet 10 inches) thick are used, allowing vaulters to fall from heights of five meters (16.4 feet) or more.

LIVE TARGETS
FACT #18

Hundreds of Pigeons Killed at 1900 Games

Throughout the history of the Summer Games a variety of new events have been introduced: many have become popular, must-see fixtures of the Olympic lineup while others have flopped and were never included again. On the short list for the most epic failure of them all—and certainly the bloodiest of anything that has been tried through the years—is an event that took place in 1900 at the Paris Games.

Shooting events have been a part of the Olympics since the beginning and have featured competitors using bows, pistols, and rifles to fire at a variety of targets. But in Paris, live pigeons were used as targets. One by one competitors would take a turn, getting in position with their rifle. A live pigeon would be released, and the competitor would attempt to shoot it out of the air. Shooters were eliminated once they missed two shots. The total number of birds they shot determined the winners. More than 300 pigeons were reportedly killed during the event.

Two events were held, each with a different entry fee, as prize money was distributed to the winners. Donald Mackintosh of Australia and Leon de Lunden of Belgium were the

TODAY'S TARGET: CLAY PIGEONS

Today competitors fire at clay disks, known as "pigeons." At the 2020 Games there will be trap and skeet shooting. In skeet shooting, competitors shoot at disks released from a low house 3 feet off the ground and a high house 10 feet off the ground. In trap, shooters aim at targets launched from a series of stations partially underground.

winners, shooting 22 and 21 pigeons, respectively.

As one can imagine, seeing live pigeons shot in rapid succession horrified many spectators and there was plenty of backlash. The event was eliminated and remains the only time in Olympic history that something living was killed on purpose.

DUMMY DEER

For the shooting events at the London Games in 1908, competitors shot at deer—which were actually cutouts shaped like the animal with targets painted on them. The targets were different sizes with different point values. Shooters had 10 attempts to hit the moving target with a rifle from a distance of 110 yards (100 meters).

RUNNING THROUGH TRAFFIC FACT #19

Keino Runs a Mile to Stadium to Make the Race

Kipchoge "Kip" Keino's journey to long-distance running greatness, and his first Olympic gold medal, began on a traffic-choked street in Mexico City during the 1968 Summer Games. The bus Keino was riding in to the Olympic Stadium had ground to a stop in a bumper-to-bumper jam, and the finals of the 1,500 meters were starting within an hour. So he got off and jogged a mile to the stadium.

It should be noted that this man had already been suffering from stomach pains that would turn out to be a gallbladder infection. A few days earlier Keino had collapsed late in the finals of the 10,000 meters under the cruel high altitude conditions of Mexico City and he had to race a throng of world-class runners in the 1,500 meters, headlined by American great and gold medal favorite Jim Ryun, who hadn't been beaten at this distance in three years.

Keino, unbothered by the unplanned warm-up run to get to the stadium, ran an Olympic-record time of 3:34.91 to win the gold medal, finishing nearly 3 seconds ahead of Ryun at 3:37.89. Keino also won a silver medal in the 5,000 meters, narrowly missing out on a gold. His performances ushered in the beginning of African dominance in the long-distance events that remains as strong as ever these days.

Four years later at the Summer Games in Munich, the Kenyan showed off his running prowess by winning the 3,000-meter steeplechase with an Olympic-record time, along with grabbing a silver medal in the 1,500 meters.

> "When I started at primary school, I ran in my bare feet four miles to school in the morning, home for lunch, again for afternoon school and back at the end of the day. I did this every day until I left school."
>
> — Kip Keino

Kenya's Kip Keino outdueled American great Jim Ryun to win the 1,500 meters at the 1968 Summer Games in Mexico City, setting an Olympic record in the process.

SILVER RUSH
FACT #20

Olympic Gold Medals Are Barely Gold at All

It's one of the signature moments at every Summer Olympics: gold medalists with giant smiles playfully taking gentle bites of their medals on the podium for photos that will be seen worldwide. This is done in jest as a test of the metal, because real gold is a soft metal and biting it can leave teeth impressions. What exactly are these newly crowned Olympic champions really sinking their teeth into though?

Well, it's not quite gold. Surprisingly, the gold medals that are draped around athletes' necks every four years are composed of at least 92.5 percent silver. The host city's organizing committee decides the specific composition and design of the medals, but there are minimum standards: gold medals must be plated with at least 6 grams of gold and they must be at least 3 millimeters thick and 60 millimeters (27.2 inches) in diameter. Silver medals contain the same amount of silver as the gold medals, with copper mixed in. Bronze medals are typically composed of mostly copper, with small traces of zinc and tin.

Beginning in 1928 medals featured Nike, the Greek Goddess of Victory, holding a palm in her left hand and a crown in her right hand on one side of the medal,

PODIUM PRESENTATIONS

The custom of awarding gold, silver, and bronze medals to the top three finishers in an Olympic event began with the 1904 Games in St. Louis. At the first modern Olympic Games in Athens in 1896, silver medals were presented to the winners and second place received a bronze medal. At the 1900 Games in Paris, trophies were handed out to the winners.

while the flip side had a crowd carrying the champion with a stadium in the background. Through the years organizing committees have come up with their own designs, as the medals handed out at the 2016 Rio Games had the Goddess of Victory flying into the stadium on one side while the flip side of the medal featured laurel leaves, which were a symbol of victory in ancient Greece.

GILDED PRIZE

The last Olympic gold medals that were made from solid gold were handed out at the 1912 Stockholm Games. All future Olympiads featured gold medals that were silver with gold plating. Before 1960, medals were designed to be pinned to the athlete's chest, rather than placed around his or her neck.

REPRESENTATIVE RINGS
FACT #21

Olympic Ring Colors Come from National Flags

From Argentina and Austria to Zambia and Zimbabwe, and every country in between, they are all represented by one of the most recognizable symbols on the planet: the Olympic rings. Five perfectly interconnected rings—blue, black, and red on the top row; yellow and green underneath, positioned on a white background—with at least one of those colors appearing on every national flag that is marched into the opening ceremonies every four years by athletes anxious to compete on the world stage at the Summer Olympics.

Pierre de Coubertin, founder of the IOC and referred to as the father of the modern Olympic Games, created the symbol largely by accident. Following the 1912 Summer Games in Stockholm, Sweden, which were the first to have athletes from North and South America, Europe, Africa, Asia, and Australia competing together, he was inspired by the momentous occasion and drew five interlocking circles at the top of a letter he composed to a colleague.

De Coubertin linked the rings to represent a world that is unified and connected by many of the Olympic values, such as teamwork and fitness. De Coubertin used the design as the emblem for the IOC's

20th anniversary celebration in 1914. World War I caused the cancellation of the 1916 Games, so the rings debuted at the 1920 Games in Antwerp, Belgium.

More than a century later, the Olympic rings stand as one of the world's most recognizable designs and a symbol of a united world coming together to celebrate the far-reaching and never-ending power of sports in our lives.

"These five rings represent the five parts of the world now won over to the cause of Olympism and ready to accept its fecund rivalries. What is more, the six colors thus combined reproduce those of all nations without exception."
— Pierre de Coubertin

The Olympic Rings, created by Pierre de Coubertin following the 1912 Summer Olympics in Stockholm, are an iconic symbol and are recognized worldwide.

ART AWARDS
FACT #22

Painting Used to Be an Olympic Event

During the first half of the 20th century, great speed, strength, or agility weren't needed to capture an Olympic medal. Those with no athletic ability, but skilled with a paintbrush and understanding of color schemes, could also contend for medals.

That's because beginning with the 1912 Summer Games in Stockholm, art categories for painting, literature, music, sculpture, and architecture were introduced. Pierre de Coubertin, recognized as the father of the modern Olympic Games, believed that part of being a true Olympian meant being skilled in the arts too, but his desire to have these events included in the Summer Games was met with great resistance early on. Stockholm organizers relented, and Italy's Giovanni Pellegrini won the first Olympic painting gold medal.

From the beginning, the events generated little interest. Rules dictated that all artwork must tie into some aspect of the Olympic concept, so there were numerous paintings depicting athletic events. A panel of judges evaluated each painting, which made scoring dicey since viewing art is incredibly subjective. Plus, only amateurs were allowed to

FAMILY FOCUSED ON THE ARTS

Jack Butler Yeats won a silver medal in painting at the 1924 Summer Games for an oil canvas he did entitled "The Liffy Swim." He was the brother of famous Irish poet William Butler Yeats, a Nobel Prize winner and one of the most important figures in 20th century literature.

compete, so the world's great artists, like Pablo Picasso or Jackson Pollock, weren't eligible.

Arts events were eliminated after the 1948 London Games. Great Britain's Alfred Thomson, a deaf painter, won the last Olympic painting gold medal. The medals won in these events are no longer counted in the official Olympic medal tables.

ARTISTIC QUINTET

The five Olympic art events were referred to as the "Pentathlon of the Muses." The arts do live on at the Olympics. Today, each organizing committee puts on a Cultural Olympiad, which is a "program of cultural events that serve to promote harmonious relations, mutual understanding and friendship among the participants."

DUCK-CROSSING DELAY
FACT #23

Rower Stops Racing Due to Crossing Ducks

During the single sculls event at the 1928 Amsterdam Games, Henry "Bobby" Pearce's world-best rowing skills, beloved personality, and top-notch character were on full display. The best rower of his era, this native of Sydney, Australia, was facing France's Vincent Saurin in the quarterfinals of the lung-searing and shoulder-pulverizing 2,000-meters race. The loser of the race would return home medal-less while the winner would move into the final four, where three of those would claim medals. So, there was a lot at stake in the race. Plus, Saurin was no slouch: he had won nine national titles and medaled three times at the European Championships.

Pearce, as he often did, powered to an early lead in the race. Around the halfway mark he spotted a duck and her ducklings slowly swimming in a single file line across the water. With the race up for grabs, Pearce came to a stop and allowed the ducks to pass. Meanwhile, Saurin kept rowing and soon overtook him. By the time the ducks had moved on and Pearce had resumed rowing, he found himself in the unfamiliar position of trailing by several scull lengths.

But over the final few hundred meters he chewed up the deficit with powerful strokes and propelled himself to a cushy 29-second victory.

In the finals, without any unplanned stops to make, he beat American Kenneth Myers with a world record time of 7:11.0 that was so ridiculously fast that it remained untouchable in the record books for 44 years.

> "It's funny now, but it wasn't at the time for I had to lean on my oars and wait for a clear course, and all the while my opponent was pulling away to a five-length lead."
>
> — Bobby Pearce

Australian rowing great Bobby Pearce stopped to allow ducklings to pass during a race at the 1924 Summer Olympics and still went on to win a gold medal.

HEROIC HUNGARIAN FACT #24

Shooter Wins Gold Using His Off Hand

While going through army training exercises in 1938, Hungary's world-class marksman Károly Takács lost the use of his right hand in a grenade explosion, but he didn't allow the grisly life-changing moment to shatter his longtime dream of winning Olympic gold.

After spending a month in the hospital recovering, Takács went to work teaching himself how to shoot left-handed, something he had never done before. He practiced for many months in private and he was soon rewarded for his tenacity. A year after suffering the injury he showed up and won the Hungarian National Pistol Shooting Championship.

Back in 1936, despite being one of the best pistol marksmen in the world, Takács was deprived of a spot on Hungary's team for the Olympics in Berlin because team rules only allowed commissioned officers to compete and, as a sergeant, he wasn't eligible. So in 1940 when Hungarian officials lifted that ban, the path for him to shoot at the 1940 Olympics appeared wide open. World War II would derail those dreams though—wiping out both the 1940 and 1944 Games.

SUPREME SHOOTING

Takács' shooting skills showed no signs of decline four years later at the 1952 Summer Games in Helsinki, Finland, as his gold medal-winning score of 579 points in the 25-meter rapid-fire pistol event was just one point shy of his winning score at the London Games. He nipped teammate Szilard Kun, who finished a point behind for the silver medal.

When the 1948 London Games arrived, the 38-year-old Takács stunned the field by not only showing up but also winning the gold medal that he had dreamed about for so long—shooting left-handed. His score of 580 points in the men's 25-meter rapid-fire pistol event was nine better than Argentina's Carlos Enrique Diaz Saenz Valiente, the reigning world champion and world-record holder.

GOODBYE TO THE GAMES

The Melbourne Games in 1956 were Takács' Olympic farewell, as he finished in eighth place with 575 points. Romania's Stefan Petrescu won the gold medal with 587 points. Takács' countryman and student Szilárd Kun finished sixth, earning three more points than his teacher.

GOT YOU AGAIN
FACT #25

Soviet Caught Using Self-Scoring Sword

At the Opening Ceremonies of every Olympic Games, one athlete is selected to read the Athlete's Oath, which says, in part:

I promise that we shall take part in these Olympic Games, respecting and abiding by the rules which govern them, in the true spirit of sportsmanship

The great majority of athletes are faithful to this oath. Then there are those that adhere to a different oath: If you're not cheating, you're not trying.

In 1976, fencer Boris Onischenko of the Soviet Union tried a way around the rules that was unique to his sport. He was competing in the modern pentathlon, a unique event that combines five disciplines, assigning points for the results in each to determine an overall winner. The events are:

- Equestrian
- Fencing
- Shooting
- Swimming
- Cross-country

In the fencing portion of the event, athletes use swords called épées, which electronically register a point when the tip is depressed in making contact with the opponent. During the competition, the team from Great Britain grew suspicious of Onischenko's prowess in an

CATCHY MONIKER

The press at the time had a field day with this story. Onischenko, who won a silver medal in the pentathlon at the 1972 Munich Games, cost his Russian teammates a shot at their own Olympic medals as they were disqualified from the team competition. English-language newspaper headlines around the world dubbed him "Dis-onischenko".

earlier bout with one of its members. Jim Fox was the next British athlete to face Onischenko, and during their bout there came a point where Onischenko scored when Fox was adamant that he had not been touched. Officials confiscated Onischenko's épée and discovered that he had rigged his weapon to send a scoring signal by hitting a switch in the grip. He was kicked out of the Olympics and banned from the sport for life.

NATIONAL DISGRACE

The Soviets did not take this incident well. Rumors swirled that the Soviet volleyball team confronted Onischenko and tried to toss him through a window. Upon his return to the Soviet Union, he was reportedly called in front of the Soviet president for a personal tongue-lashing. He was then fined 5,000 rubles and dishonorably discharged from the army.

SWIMMER TO STAR
FACT #26

Star Olympic Swimmer Became Movie Icon

One of the greatest swimmers ever pulled off one of the rarest feats of all: becoming an Olympic champion and a Hollywood icon. Chicago's Johnny Weissmuller, winner of five gold medals, was even better in the jungle, the setting for a dozen of the popular Tarzan movies he starred in during the 1930s and 1940s.

Weissmuller splashed onto the Olympic scene at the 1924 Paris Olympics and showed that he was already a star on the rise. He won gold medals in the 100- and 400-meter freestyle and 800-meter relay. His epic win in a showdown with teammate, rival, and surfing great Duke Kahanamoku in the 100 meters remains one of the greatest races in the history of swimming. Weissmuller also played on the U.S. water polo team that won a bronze medal. He even found time to entertain spectators, as he and teammate Stubby Kruger performed humorous diving routines between events.

By the 1928 Summer Games, Weissmuller was an international star, having performed exhibitions throughout Europe. He carried the U.S. flag at the opening ceremonies and won gold medals in the 100-meter freestyle and 4x200-meter relay.

In 1932, the movie *Tarzan the Ape Man* was a giant hit with audiences and critics both in the United States and internationally. The Tarzan movies were based on books about an infant raised by apes in the jungle. In 1956, Weissmuller starred in the television series Jungle Jim where he was a hunter, guide, and explorer in Africa. He has a star on the Hollywood Walk of Fame.

"**The public forgives my acting because they know I was an athlete. They know I wasn't make-believe.**"

— Johnny Weissmuller

Johnny Weissmuller's rivalry with Duke Kahanamoku started at the 1924 Summer Olympics, where they dueled in one of the greatest races ever, and Weissmuller then continued into movie making.

SWIMMING WITH TARZAN

(SWIMMING WITH TARZAN PARIS 1924 L ▶ F C GAMES)

NICE FLAG
FACT #27

Two Countries Once Showed Up with the Same Flag

Admirers of the flag of the small European nation of Liechtenstein have the 1936 Olympic Games in Berlin to thank.

The original flag of Liechtenstein dates back to the 18th century and had a simple design: a gold-colored band above an equal-sized red band. In 1852, the design and colors were changed. Instead of vertical bands, the country decided on two equal-sized horizontal blocks. They kept the red (on the left) but made the right side block blue.

Fifteen years before the Berlin Olympics, Liechtenstein changed its flag design from equal horizontal blocks back to equal vertical bands, with red on the bottom again. If only the decision had been made to just keep the yellow, or that red should get a chance to be on top, Liechtenstein would have avoided a somewhat embarrassing Olympic debut at the 1936 Opening Ceremonies in Berlin. To the surprise of the Liechtensteiners, (and in a déjà vu moment for spectators) their new flag was identical to the flag that Haiti had marched under just moments before.

As it turns out, Haiti's flag dates back to the mid-19th century, but has not changed since. Haitians celebrate Haitian Flag Day

NOT THAT IT MATTERED

It was unlikely that the identical flags were going to be an issue outside of the Opening Ceremonies. The chance of seeing the two flags side by side at a medal ceremony were slim as the countries had just seven athletes between them. Haiti's only athlete dropped out before his event, and the Liechtenstein athletes had poor prospects for winning medals.

annually on May 18th. After Liechtenstein made the switch in 1921, without the Internet or even widespread color photography, the flags of these two small nations had never been compared.

In 1937, Liechtenstein addressed the issue when it added a gold-colored crown to the top left corner of its flag.

PUNY PRINCIPALITY

Liechtenstein is one of the world's smallest countries at just 62 square miles (160 square kilometers), which is just a little smaller than Washington, D.C. With a population of less than 40,000 people, the tiny nation has never produced an Olympic Summer Games medalist. It has, however, won 10 Winter Games medals, including two gold by skier Hanni Wenzel.

SLEEPING SPEEDSTER
FACT #28

U.S. Sprinter Awakes from Coma to Win Gold

In 1928, Chicago-area native Betty Robinson was the fastest woman in the world. Three years later, she could not get out of bed. This epic Olympic saga started in early 1928, when the 16-year-old Robinson won the first 100-meter race she ever ran. The next time she ran the race was in early July of that year, when she won the U.S. Olympic trials.

In late July, just weeks before her 17th birthday, Robinson became the first woman to win an Olympic gold medal in the 100-meters. The first year that the IOC allowed women to compete in track and field was 1928 in Amsterdam. Back home in Chicago, Robinson set the world record in the 100-yard dash in September. She enrolled at Northwestern University the next year and kept running at record pace, setting a world-best mark in the 50-yard dash in 1929. Two years later she set two more world records, in the 60- and 70-yard dashes. The teenager was on top of the world until tragedy struck.

In 1931, Robinson was involved in a plane crash that caused severe injuries and left her in a coma. It was seven months before she woke up. For six more months Robinson was confined to a

ATHLETIC PIONEERS

Modern Olympics founder Pierre de Coubertin was vehemently opposed to female participation at the Games. He argued that his vision was to replicate the Olympics of ancient Greece, where women did not compete. De Coubertin allowed for traditional female sports of the day such as golf and tennis, which women first took part in at the 1900 Games in Paris. Female participation in track and field only began after de Coubertin resigned from the IOC in 1925.

wheelchair. She then fought to get back to her athletic peak, missing the 1932 Olympics in Los Angeles as she recuperated.

With a lot of hard work, Robinson came back to qualify for the 1936 Berlin Games as a member of the 4x100-meter relay team. She ran the third leg as the Americans beat Great Britain for the gold medal.

FIRST CHAMPION

Poland's Halina Konopacka was the first woman in history to win an Olympic gold medal in track and field. She was the champion of the discus throw event at the 1928 Amsterdam Games with a world-record toss of 39.62 meters (130 feet). Later in life, Konopacka was a writer and an artist. After her death in 1989, she was awarded the Silver Cross of Merit, the highest civilian award in Poland.

DISQUALIFIED IN DISGRACE
FACT #29

Winners Kicked Out of Badminton Event

The Summer Olympics have been a long-running showcase of what makes sports in society so incredibly special: passionate athletes competing with integrity, heart, and a never-give-up spirit that inspires. Unfortunately, there has also been plenty of ugly behavior that has tarnished events and destroyed athletes' reputations as well.

As recently as at the 2012 London Games, four pairs of women's doubles badminton players were booted from their event for tanking matches in a disgraceful and, as it turned out, disastrous attempt at manipulating the tournament draw and securing more favorable matches in the knockout round. The top-seeded Chinese team, two teams from South Korea, and a team from Indonesia were all sent packing.

Yu Yang

The Chinese team of Yu Yang and Wang Xiaoli, one of the favorites to win the gold medal, played a South Korean team that was trying equally as hard not to win. Both were trying to avoid playing the second seeded Chinese team of Tian and Zhao in the next round. The spectators repeatedly booed the ludicrous non-effort. Players intentionally hit shots into the net or out of bounds, all despite repeated warnings from the referee for lackluster play.

Wang Xiac

The other South Korean team and one from Indonesia did the same in their match. Both countries appealed the disqualification, while China accepted it. The Badminton World Federation rejected the South Korean appeal and Indonesia withdrew its challenge. Four teams that had been eliminated were returned to the knockout round to replace the disqualified teams.

"**Such behavior is incompatible with the Olympic values.**"
— Mark Adams, IOC spokesman

Eight badminton players from China, South Korea, and Indonesia were expelled from the 2012 Summer Olympics for attempting to throw matches.

GROUP STAGE

This was the first time an Olympic badminton tournament had included a group stage before getting to the knockout round.

RECORD NOT ENOUGH FOR GOLD
FACT #30

World Record Leap Results in Bronze Medal

The greatest performance of Robert LeGendre's career—a world-record long jump at the 1924 Paris Olympics—earned him lots of accolades, but not a gold medal. The New York native was competing in the pentathlon, the five-event competition that featured the long jump, javelin, discus, and 200- and 1,500-meter runs. When he jumped 25 feet 6 inches (7.76 meters) in the long jump, the opening event of the pentathlon, he bettered the world record at the time of 7.69 meters (25 feet 2 inches) set by American Edward Gourdin a year earlier. The next day, the long jump competition was held, in which LeGendre hadn't qualified for. It turned out that LeGendre's jump was far better than American gold medalist DeHart Hubbard's winning leap of 7.44 meters (24 feet 5 inches).

LeGendre did depart the Paris Games with a medal though, as he won a bronze in the pentathlon. Among the 10 heats in the 200-meter run, he tied for first with the best time at 23 seconds; he was fourth in the discus; seventh in the javelin; and he ran 4:52.6 in the 1,500 meters for third place in

DENTISTRY AND DEATH

LeGendre's world record stood for nearly a year before Hubbard beat it. Following his award-filled athletic career, LeGendre went on to earn a Ph.D. and a Doctor of Dental Surgery degree from Georgetown University and practiced dentistry in the Washington, D.C., area. He died of bronchial pneumonia at age 33.

the race, which secured that position overall as well.

LeGendre was a gifted athlete and track star at Georgetown University. He finished in fourth place in the pentathlon at the 1920 Summer Olympics in Antwerp, just missing out on a medal while competing with a broken foot that wasn't completely healed. He also won the pentathlon at the Inter-Allied Athletic Games that were held in Paris at the end of World War I.

EVENT ELIMINATED

The men's pentathlon was eliminated from the Olympic lineup after the 1924 Summer Games. It was contested in three Summer Olympics. In 1912, legendary American athlete Jim Thorpe won the gold. In 1920, Missouri farm boy Brutus Hamilton was the champion (LeGendre finished fourth). In 1924, Finland's Eero Lehtonen won the last pentathlon gold medal.

GAME CHANGING EVENTS

MELBOURNE, AUSTRALIA

Seven countries boycotted these games, including the Netherlands, Switzerland, and Spain. These three were protesting Soviet military action in Hungary, a conflict that played out in competition. The IOC allowed the Soviets to compete, and in water polo they played Hungary in a semifinal match that turned violent. "Blood in the Water" screamed the headlines. Hungary won and went on to claim gold.

LONDON, UK

After six years of World War II, the world looked to war-ravaged London to pull off the first Olympics since 1936 (Germany and Japan were banned). It was not easy. These were dubbed the Austerity Games in a London that was broke. No new stadiums were built, and food was rationed, but the Games themselves were a huge success.

MUNICH, GERMANY

The 1972 Munich Games were marred b[y] attack on the Olympic Village. Palesti[nian] terrorists killed two Israeli athletes and [took] nine others hostage. The drama played [out] on live television around the worl[d. A] botched rescue attempt 20 hours later [left] all nine Israeli hostages and five of [the] terrorists dead.

POLITICS... CRISIS... SOCIAL CHANGE

OR USE BY WHITE PERSONS

HESE PUBLIC PREMISES AND THE AMENITIES
HEREOF HAVE BEEN RESERVED FOR THE
XCLUSIVE USE OF WHITE PERSONS.

By Order   Provincial Secretary

IR GEBRUIK DEUR BLANKES

HIERDIE OPENBARE PERSEEL EN DIE GERIEWE
DAARVAN IS VIR DIE UITSLUITLIKE GEBRUIK
VAN BLANKES AANGEWYS.

Op Las   Provinsiale Sekretaris

MOSCOW, USSR

In December of 1979, Soviet troops attacked the Afghan capital of Kabul, executed president Hafizullah Amin and made Babrak Karmal, who was a Soviet supporter, the new leader. This kicked off what would become a 10-year occupation. The United States led the idea of boycotting the Games if the Soviets did not withdraw, and ultimately more than 60 countries decided not to send athletes to Moscow.

MONTREAL, CANADA

ty-two African nations boycotted
1976 Montreal Games at the last
te when the IOC allowed New
and to participate after having sent
ugby team to play in South Africa.
South African government was
subject of international scorn and
tions due to its policy of racial
egation called apartheid.

RIO DE JANEIRO, BRAZIL

The IOC allowed 10 athletes without a country to participate under the Olympic flag. Amidst a worldwide refugee crisis, the IOC funded the training for the selected athletes. Examples of what they had survived include the Syrian Civil War and tribal genocide in the Democratic Republic of the Congo.

RESEARCH PROJECTS

Major moments on the world stage have impacted the Olympics through the years. The Research Projects below will bring a deeper perspective to these moments and the events that shaped them.

1. Afghanistan has been at war almost continuously since the 1979 Soviet invasion that sparked the boycott of the 1980 Moscow games. When did the three wars that have been fought since 1979 take place, and what started them?

2. The Republic of China (ROC), better known in the West as Taiwan, is one of 30 countries that boycotted the 1976 Olympics in Montreal. Unlike the other 29, however, the ROC refused to participate for a different reason. Why did the ROC pull out of the Montreal Games? How did this lead to the Nagoya Resolution? What did this resolution do, and what were the results of its establishment? Present your research in a three-column chart with the headings: ROC, Taiwan, and Chinese Taipei.

3. Research three-time Olympian and nine-time gold medalist gymnast Věra Čáslavská. She won six medals at the 1968 Games in Mexico City, but that was her last Olympic competition. Explain why Čáslavská stopped competing, what led her to take the actions that got her banned, and what happened to her in the years following the Mexico City Games.

4. Years of protests and boycotts at the Olympic games have put a spotlight on issues of politics and human rights from military invasions to apartheid. By the time the 2024 Paris Olympics roll around, the IOC will have in place a set of reforms designed to tighten rules on corruption, support environmental stability, prohibit all forms of discrimination, and adhere to United Nations standards on human rights. Research and summarize these reforms. Also look up the *Freedom in the World* report, a study by Freedom House, and list the countries that will have trouble meeting the new standards unless they make changes by 2024.

5. Doping is the term for using banned performance-enhancing substances to gain an unfair advantage in competition. Do some research to determine which countries over the years have had the most athletes fail the doping tests, and which have had the most medals stripped. Detail the sanctions issued against Russia for its state-sponsored doping program in the 2010s.

OLYMPIC GLOSSARY OF KEY TERMS

archery: the sport of shooting arrows with a bow.

banned: to prohibit, especially by legal means.

compete: to strive consciously or unconsciously for an objective (such as position, profit, or a prize).

decathlon: an athletic contest consisting of ten different track and field events.

doping: the use of a substance (such as an anabolic steroid or erythropoietin) or technique (such as blood doping) to illegally improve athletic performance.

equestrian: of, relating to, or featuring horseback riding.

heat: one of several preliminary contests held to eliminate less competent contenders.

host city: the city that is selected to be the primary location for Olympic ceremonies and events.

hurdle: a light barrier that competitors must leap over in races.

medal: a piece of metal often resembling a coin and having a stamped design that is issued to commemorate a person or event or awarded for excellence or achievement: may also mean to win a medal.

nationality: a legal relationship involving allegiance on the part of an individual and usually protection on the part of the state.

opponent: a contestant that you are matched against.

participant: a person who takes part in something.

preliminary: a minor match preceding the main event.

pommel horse: a gymnastics apparatus for swinging and balancing feats that consists of a padded rectangular or cylindrical form with two handgrips called pommels on the top and that is supported in a horizontal position above the floor.

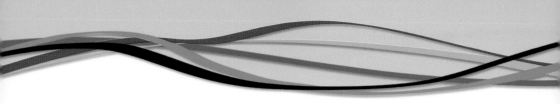

qualify: meet the required standard.

referee: the official in a sport who is expected to ensure fair play.

repechage: a race (especially in rowing) in which runners-up in the eliminating heats compete for a place in the final race.

spectator: one who looks on or watches.

sportsmanship: fairness, honesty, and courtesy in following the rules of a game.

stamina: enduring strength and energy.

standings: an ordered listing of scores or results showing the relative positions of competitors (individuals or teams) in an event.

substitute: a player or competitor that takes the place of another.

torch: a cylindrical or cone-shaped object in which the Olympic flame is ceremonially carried.

vault: to execute a leap using the hands or a pole.

venue: the place where any event or action is held.

victory: a successful ending of a struggle or contest; a win.

EDUCATIONAL VIDEO LINKS

#4: American Wins Marathon Running Just 14 Miles: http://x-qr.net/1L5Q
#5: Athletes Can Win Olympic Medals by Walking: http://x-qr.net/1LMr
#7: Boxing Referee Assaulted at Seoul Games: http://x-qr.net/1Kp0
#12: Ethiopian Wins 1960 Marathon Running Without Shoes:
  http://x-qr.net/1LFa
#15: Fujimoto Wins Gold Medal with Broken Knee: http://x-qr.net/1K52
#19: Keino Runs a Mile to Stadium to Make the Race: http://x-qr.net/1KSx
#21: Olympic Ring Colors Come From National Flags: http://x-qr.net/1M9G
#23: Rower Stops Racing Due to Crossing Ducks: http://x-qr.net/1L1C
#26: Star Olympic Swimmer Became Movie Icon: http://x-qr.net/1KE3
#29: Winners Kicked Out of Badminton Event: http://x-qr.net/1M1x

The Summer Olympics: Fascinating Facts

FURTHER READING

Burns, Bob. *The Track in the Forest: The Creation of a Legendary 1968 U.S. Olympic Team.* Chicago: Chicago Review Press, 2018.

Hart, Eddie. *Disqualified: Eddie Hart, Munich 1972, and the Voices of the Most Tragic Olympics.* Kent: The Kent State University Press/Black Squirrel Books, 2017.

Hoffer, Richard. *Something in the Air: American Passion and Defiance in the 1968 Mexico City Olympics.* Lincoln: University of Nebraska Press, 2018.

McGill, Steven. *A Hurdler's Hurdler: The Life of Rodney Milburn, Olympic Champion.* Jefferson: McFarland and Company, 2018.

Welch, Bob. *The Wizard of Foz: Dick Fosbury's One-Man High Jump Revolution.* New York: Skyhorse Publishing, 2018.

INTERNET RESOURCES

www.olympic.org/
The official website of the IOC. The site features the latest news and information regarding the Olympics, an archive of results and photos from past Olympic Games, and information on the IOC and its members.

www.teamusa.org/
The official website of the United States Olympic & Paralympic Committee. Included on this site are profiles of Team USA athletes and the latest news and results from competitions involving U.S. athletes worldwide. Plus, there is a real-time clock counting down to the start of the 2020 Summer Olympics in Tokyo.

www.nbcolympics.com/
The website of NBC Sports, which is covering the 2020 Summer Olympics. A breakdown of all the events that will be contested in Tokyo are included, along with the latest Olympic news from around the world.

www.olympicchannel.com/en/
The official website of the Olympic Channel. The site features profiles of past and present Olympians, access to original programming, and the latest news and information regarding the Olympics.

www.espn.com/olympics/
This web page is ESPN's coverage of everything related to the Olympics, including all the latest news and information regarding Olympic athletes from around the world.

https://www.penn.museum/sites/olympics/olympicorigins.shtml
Produced by the University of Pennsylvania Museum of Archaeology and Anthropology, the site features information on the ancient Olympic Games, its athletes, and the politics that surrounded them.

INDEX

PHOTO CREDITS

Shutterstock.com: Eastimages: 7, kovop58: 9, Sportpoint: 40, Leonard Zhukovsky: 73

Dreamstime.com: Chelsdo: 12, Jessica Kirsh: 16, Jerry Coli: 24, Lucian Milasan: 28, Kai Shen: 38, Marcos Souza: 44, Fotostraveller: 46, Paul Vinten: 32, Romantiche: 52, 9dreamstudio: 54, cover (bottom) Kutizoltan

Wikimedia Commons: IOC Olympic Museum/Public domain: 14, Public domain: 18, 26, 30, 34, 64, 66, 70 MSGT Lono Kollars: 20, RIA Novosti archive Vitaliy Saveliev: 22, Louis Melsheimer: 42, Mitch Ames: 50, Fairfax Media: 56, Karoly by Kingrulz64: 58, U.S. Army: 60, George Grantham Bainderivative work Entheta: 62, Tom Page: 68, National Media Museum from UK: 72, Thaler Tamas: 72, High Contrast: 72, Dewet: 73, NFYFLY: 73

Alamy Stock Photos: INTERFOTO: 36, The Print Collector: 48

All background images provided by Shutterstock and Dreamstime

AUTHOR BIOGRAPHY

GREG BACH is the author of 10 books, including titles on sports and coaching. Growing up in Swartz Creek, Michigan, he has been a lifelong fan of the Detroit Tigers and has fond memories of attending games with his family at the old Tiger Stadium. He is a proud graduate of Michigan State University and resides in West Palm Beach, Florida.